Ey Help for
a Happy
Retirement

Elf-help for a Happy Retirement

written by
Ted O'Neal

illustrated by
R.W. Alley

ONE
CARING
PLACE

Abbey Press

Text © 2001 by Ted O'Neal
Illustrations © 2001 by St. Meinrad Archabbey
Published by One Caring Place
Abbey Press
St. Meinrad, Indiana 47577

Library of Congress Catalog Number
2001089653

ISBN 0-87029-354-0

Printed in the United States of America

Foreword

Many of us define ourselves—who we are—by "what we do for a living," or "what we used to do." But the truth is that when we retire, we are still the same people we always were; we don't need to feel as though we are surrendering our very selves. It is only our circumstances that have changed.

Preparing for, adapting to, and making the most of these new circumstances is what *Elf-help for a Happy Retirement* is all about. Author Ted O'Neal and illustrator R.W. Alley offer provocative and practical pointers on topics ranging from how to stay active, to how to keep growing, and where to turn in times of stress or fear or loss.

In the end, the message rings through loud and clear: No matter the circumstances, this is a time for new beginnings.

1.

Congratulations! You have reached a milestone that proclaims accomplishment, achievement, arrival—and possibility.

2.

It is time to recognize that
your past is invaluable,
and your future is precious.
But don't forget your present.
Now is sacred time, too.

3.

This can be a time for you to choose life's tempo. While many of life's commitments remain, you may be able to linger a little longer in the hammock or easy chair—if that's what suits you. Retirement can mean a new schedule for your activities—and inactivities.

4.

Studies show that people get psychologically healthier as they grow older. Like cheese and wine that get better with age, now is the time to become that better-balanced person you've always wanted to be.

5.

One myth about retirement is that life suddenly becomes "a ball" or "a bowl-full of cherries," or a "permanent vacation." Still another myth is that retirement is boring. While you may find your new life "all of the above" at times, remember: Life doesn't need to be perfect to be wonderful.

6.

Your new freedom can be
a terrifying thing. Despite
less pressure and fewer
responsibilities, you still
need a good reason to get
out of bed in the mornings.
Be sure to keep on dreaming
and setting goals for yourself.
We grow old only when we
lose our enthusiasm and
our ideals.

7.

Our society suggests that "useful" and "productive" equals "good," that "beautiful" equals "young." And yet we know that some of the most beautiful people in the world are frail and weathered in body, but not in spirit and heart. Radiate beauty, no matter your physical condition or amount of "productivity"!

8.

Retirees often define themselves by just how busy they still are. The busier we are, the more important we must be! Don't underestimate the value of simple contemplation.

9.

As a working person, you may have seen yourself as a "provider." As a retired person, you are now *a different kind of provider:* Now you can provide love, care, time, example.

10.

Don't underestimate the value of the example you are giving everyone—your grandchildren, your neighbors, your community—when you show tolerance, or mercy, or forgiveness, or generosity, or patience. It's never too late in life to be an inspiration to someone!

11.

Fitness, of course, is not just for young folks. We don't retire from the need to keep our minds and bodies active and energized. It's never too late to begin— or to begin again. And it's important to know that even a little bit of activity can make a lot of difference.

Walking
Path

12.

Family is always important—no matter what definition we may have for family. Above all, it means having good relationships. Treasure these and build upon them.

13.

"It is not how old we are, but how we are old," goes one popular saying. If we can still be creative, still be purposeful, still be trusting and hopeful and enthusiastic, we can still be happy.

14.

In your working life you "kept your edge" by always learning new techniques, new processes, new tricks of the trade. Keep your edge now by continuing to make learning a lifelong pursuit.

15.

Developing new interests has always been a life-enhancer. Remember when you first discovered cross-stitching, or chess, or line-dancing, or Mozart? New skills, new directions, new interests keep our joints and our spirits operating "like new."

16.

Studies show that as we
age we get more dependable,
more compassionate, more
straightforward in dealing
with others, more prone to
finish what we started, more
perceptive to the needs of others.
Further developing these
wonderful traits is the noble
"work" of the retirement years.

17.

Now may be the time to "take up the cause" that's always been in the back of your mind. Volunteering your experience and wisdom will bring rewards for both giver and receiver.

18.

Many people continue working part-time during their retirement. It "keeps them going" while bringing in extra income. Whether you choose to be retired or semi-retired, the important thing is to keep a "never-too-tired" attitude.

19.

Humor helps everything. Stay young at heart by being playful. There are opportunities for lightheartedness all around!

20.

Ancient wisdom has it that only three things are necessary for happiness: Something to do; someone to love; something to look forward to. Make sure that with each new sunrise your day is open to all three of these simple necessities.

21.

You may find yourself missing the routines of the workaday world. You can get yourself into a satisfying new rhythm by starting up new patterns. Having a routine turns your day into a series of stepping stones, helping you know what's next, forcing you to keep moving and motivated.

22.

Loneliness can become a part of anyone's life—but especially for those who find themselves "out of the loop" for the first time. While many kind souls may try to keep you "connected," it's primarily your own task to keep reaching out.

23.

Many retired people make their church, their faith community, a very important part of their lives. People of faith can help you keep your soul alive when your spirits wane. And, just the same, you can bring a spiritual pick-me-up to others when they need it most.

24.

Tending to our souls is more important than even our bodies. That means tending to our relationships—something that will never diminish like our bodies will. No matter how aching our bodies or how severe our losses, we can be sustained by strong relationships with ourselves, our neighbors, our family, our God.

25.

Retirement means having time to pray—no excuses. The thing to remember is that a big part of prayer is what God does—not what we do. Practice the art of listening, of being present, of being open and receptive.

26.

Now that you know what matters in life—what is really important and what is not—you may find yourself less inhibited, less reluctant to say or show your love and your true spirit. Working on this "serenity of spirit" and sharing it is your new full-time job.

27.

Seeking help with problems is an act of courage. If your eyes need glasses, your ears need an aid, your legs need wheels, admit to this need and go out and get them.

28.

You will encounter special stresses as you confront the normal losses of aging—the death of a friend or loved one, a new physical limitation, fears about your health or the health of someone you care about. Find someone, or a group, who can be your "cheering section" when you're down. (And you can be theirs when *they* need a lift.)

29.

Have fun! Make it a part of your daily schedule. Everyone's spirits need lifting once in awhile, and putting "fun" on your calendar will give you something to look forward to and help you feel good about yourself and helping others.

30.

Today's retired people don't lie under a tree and play checkers—unless they want to. Everyone wants to be productive, contributing, achieving this and accomplishing that... but only up to a point!

31.

The subject of "enough money" is a part of any retirement planning or discussion. And it's an important part. But don't let economics be your only guide to what to do. Some of the best things in life are free.

32.

Regrets: There will always be some. And there will always be one more person to forgive. This person may even be yourself!

33.

Now may be the time to reconnect, to renew, to reestablish old relationships. If some of them are due for a "patching up," so much the better. It's a challenge that will be worth the price.

34.

If you are lonely or hurting or worried, know that you are not alone. Share your sacred bond with others who will benefit by your company and compassion. You are sure to receive even more than you give.

ELF HOLLOW
NURSING HOME

35.

Should boredom become an issue, resort to the old-fashioned remedies: letters to friends and relatives; a good, long novel or biography of someone you admire (maybe even an autobiography!); a recipe or craft or project with a beginning, a middle, and an end. Dive in and begin!

36.

Invite people into your home: people who are like you, as well as those who are not. While the former will help you be yourself, the latter may help you stretch into who you'd like to become!

37.

It can be a rewarding exercise to tend to our memories, do a life review, and be proud and thankful for all that has been. But it is good to look forward, too. As one poet advised: We should not live each day as if it were our last—but as if it were our first. The best is yet to be!

38.

No matter how much planning
we do, we can never really
know what is ahead for us.
Trust that God knows—and
cares—and will never retire
from that loving work.

Ted O'Neal is the author of *Garden Therapy*, and along with his daughter, Jenny, author of the *Elf-help for Kids* book, *Respect: Dare to Care, Share, and Be Fair.* He has been known to receive a senior-citizen discount on occasion.

Illustrator for the Abbey Press Elf-help Books, **R.W. Alley** also illustrates and writes children's books. He lives in Barrington, Rhode Island, with his wife, daughter, and son.

The Story of the Abbey Press Elves

The engaging figures that populate the Abbey Press "elf-help" line of publications and products first appeared in 1987 on the pages of a small self-help book called *Be-good-to-yourself Therapy*. Shaped by the publishing staff's vision and defined in R.W. Alley's inventive illustrations, they lived out author Cherry Hartman's gentle, self-nurturing advice with charm, poignancy, and humor.

Reader response was so enthusiastic that more Elf-help Books were soon under way, a still-growing series that has inspired a line of related gift products.

The especially endearing character featured in the early books—sporting a cap with a mood-changing candle in its peak—has since been joined by a spirited female elf with flowers in her hair.

These two exuberant, sensitive, resourceful, kindhearted, lovable sprites, along with their lively elfin community, reveal what's truly important as they offer messages of joy and wonder, playfulness and co-creation, wholeness and serenity, the miracle of life and the mystery of God's love.

With wisdom and whimsy, these little creatures with long noses demonstrate the elf-help way to a rich and fulfilling life.

Elf-help Books

...adding "a little character" and a lot
of help to self-help reading!

Stress Therapy	#20153
Making-sense-out-of-suffering Therapy	#20156
Get Well Therapy	#20157
Anger Therapy	#20127
Caregiver Therapy	#20164
Self-esteem Therapy	#20165
Take-charge-of-your-life Therapy	#20168
Work Therapy	#20166
Everyday-courage Therapy	#20167
Peace Therapy	#20176
Friendship Therapy	#20174
Christmas Therapy (color edition) $5.95	#20175
Grief Therapy	#20178
Happy Birthday Therapy	#20181
Forgiveness Therapy	#20184
Keep-life-simple Therapy	#20185
Celebrate-your-womanhood Therapy	#20189
Acceptance Therapy (color edition) $5.95	#20182
Acceptance Therapy	#20190

Keeping-up-your-spirits Therapy	#201
Play Therapy	#20
Slow-down Therapy	#20203
One-day-at-a-time Therapy	#20204
Prayer Therapy	#20206
Be-good-to-your-marriage Therapy	#20205
Be-good-to-yourself Therapy (hardcover) $10.95	#20196
Be-good-to-yourself Therapy	#20255

Book price is $4.95 unless otherwise noted.
Available at your favorite giftshop or bookstore—
or directly from One Caring Place, Abbey Press
Publications, St. Meinrad, IN 47577.
Or call 1-800-325-2511.